WOMEN COME TO A DEATH

WOMEN COME TO A DEATH

Dilys Wood

KATABASIS

First published in 1997 by KATABASIS
10 St Martins Close, London NW1 0HR (0171 485 3830)
Copyright: Dilys Wood 1997
Printed and bound by Antony Rowe Ltd, Chippenham (01249 659705)
The front cover illustration is a detail from a picture in the poet's collection, photographed by Roger Smith.
The back cover shows a framed photo of the poet's mother on a table by a bowl of fruit, photographed by Roger Smith.
Typeset in-house mainly in 12 point Albertus.

Trade Distribution: Password Books
23 New Mount Street
Manchester M4 4DE (0161 953 4009)

ISBN: 0 904872 28 9

KATABASIS is grateful for the support
of the London Arts Board.

CONTENTS

I

II

III

IV

I

DEATH OF A SAFETY OFFICER

The poem concerns Eddie, an imaginary character based on a real person, who worked in a South Yorkshire pit for many years as Safety Officer, and a group of women visiting the dying man in hospital. Called 'Chorus' for convenience, the women might be thought of as sometimes speaking as a group, sometimes singly or in pairs. The setting is a side-ward in a modern hospital on the outskirts of a city. It is afternoon, New Year's Day, 1996.

DEATH OF A SAFETY OFFICER

Eddie

> Do not hasten me dying,
> and do not slow me —
> I know it by the faces
> that do not know me.

Chorus

> Where is he? Is this he?
> I cannot look.
>
> In this receptacle
> of bone, horn, skin,
> ashen light burns
> through paper-thin walls.

Eddie

> Theirs the haste,
> but not the timing.
>
> An oval face,
> like her mother's, turns
> from a stranger dying.

Chorus

> Tears on his face.
> An urn overflows.
>
> I've come in haste,
> rushed, as ever, by the telephone —
> wanting to get it over.

I've let him down,
coming without make-up,
with old clothes on,
without even a comb
through my hair — scurfed
with the ashes of death.

Let's start again.
Take the comb and flick up the ends,
get out lipstick and blusher,
pull your jumper down
and tighten your belt —
what you've always done,
do now out of love and respect.

Eddie

Busy people slip in and out of here,
careless angels of the upper air,
but once more to the catacombs of pain,
winding down to earth's bowels once again.

Night and day have joined.
The weather's gone.
About things not understood at the time,
let me maunder on.

Chorus

His death brings back our youth.
We all go back to childhood and teens,
which takes me back to Darton School,
thoughts slipping away to Eddie's patrol
hundreds of feet below our school playground.

A lonely sentry on his safety round — six mile —
taking samples of dust
putting props to the test,
never meeting a mouse,
for, as Uncle Eddie told us,
mice stayed close
to the shafts' busy traffic and the ponies.

No-one thought to tell the little children
what their dads did,
gone off with snap-tin and water-bottle.
But Eddie was a book of stories
and so we'd follow him on his long walk
through the warren of living rock,
two hours' trek from the nearest men at work,
hearing nothing but low, uncertain sounds.

Blasting re-starts at the face,
layers of silence shift, settle,
long waves come to find him, far adrift.

Eddie

The knife-edge of indissoluble pain.

High and cold on lofty morphine.

Death brings back my youth.
Thinking only of that.
Memory turns back
into the cold flood of January air.

It dowses strong young eyes,
aches in the smooth forehead bone.

In the New Year's early dark, I make out
tall scaffolds of denser black,
the hard pierced shape of the wheels,
and another, and another,
stepped across South Yorkshire
like church spires.

The winding-gear's wakeful spirit
still turns in the wound-down light —
just enough light to see it,
never enough dark not to sense it,
a shaking glow around it
from naked bulbs strung out
in gusts wuthering
through the fouled-up site.

The last of the first unseen day winds down,
as lads come up home
under the yellow gas.
The free youth surge under the lamps,
stop in their wild play
to let the boot squad pass
and peel away.

Chorus
1st January, nineteen thirty-nine.
That was Eddie's fourteenth birthday
and first day down the pit.
Unlacing leaden boots on their back steps,
looking at his flesh tattooed wi' coal
and his barked knuckles,
he asked me, had it snowed afresh,
had the sun shone,
had we been out on us toboggans after school?

I pictured bust pipes in the school lavs,
icicles in the sun like fiery swords.
I boasted, 'I'm a good describer.
I will tell you happenings up here,
when you are in that nasty, blind hole.'

Eddie

Praise to the boiling baths, knocking like fury
in the back-boiler and nights of dancing.

Praise to the old push-bike, and free-wheel dips
of the lower Pennines. Praise strong pins

for quickstep, waltz, tango, rumba,
and the pedal back uphill,
until Kexborough and Darton

outline in the courting moon. Unhooking
house-keys from the coal-hole. Anthracite kisses!

Chorus

On a morphine drip, but see how he lies
on a thin, high ledge, too scared to budge!

A raw day. The cloud's down low.
All I can see from here
is where some drunken driver's
ploughed the grass —
his idea of bringing in New Year!

I can't stop sorrow coming in
like water through an old pair of shoes.

When we were young wives
we were not made of such thin stuff.

In the mornings, when we'd emptied the house,
our dancing partner was the wireless.

Watching his shirts fill out on the clothes-line,
who thought:
'He's two thousand feet under the earth
and there, without warning,
air's invisible web bursts into shirts of flame'?

To us the earth was 'the good earth',
the few top spit.
There a collier triple-digs
his warmed allotment in the whistling Spring —
then balances his spade across his bike,
snaps off pussy-willow and catkin twigs
rides with a bunch in his broad fist,
long danglers shaking,
cold rills of breeze blowing back
primrose-yellow clouds, fine as coal-dust,
shining on bared wrists and forearms.

He grips and peddles, sings:
'Che sarà sarà.' Whatever comes!

'Dad's brought t'spuds.
He's brought catkins for you, Mam.'
'The soppy devil! Thanks!'

Eddie

O earth! This lurching sea-berth,
voyaging from safe-ground,

propelling the pit of my stomach
through muscular waters,
stealing my sea-legs,
makes me remember your kindness.

I try to turn and lie once more
against your matching contour
on a tinder-dry, sprung heather hill-slope.

Remember us, tucked well below
the all-year-round ice-stream?
On those breezy moors, it toned down
even her body's heat . . .

In the waste of the year, at the time
of the wasting of man,
in the waste borders of this town,
call up comfort any way you can!

Chorus

This is a place for dying.
Nothing else goes on.
Surges of traffic off the M1
all that happens on New Year's Day.

Never-ending cars,
thudding like the sea, and rolling over us
like the death of a passionate man.
That's what's going on.

All his life, we've heard him called 'quiet' —
a way of speaking of his strong feelings
and his hard code.

Those who worked with him will tell you
they relied on him, but found him 'deep'.
Even now, like a banked-up fire of white cinders,
his heart could blaze up and burn us!

He stuck to his guns with bullies,
made others feel safe by his steady ways,
kept it normal.

Eddie

In the Hole we kept it normal —
putting aside the dread of flood and fire,
rotating shifts churned out coal.
Man and machine turned a single screw,
with man's whole force, forced his desire.
The black tide swelled up and out,
the earth grew emptier.

One democratic heat for a whole people,
one full grate, to set babby's tin bath,
for the old codger to jiggle his toast.

No gain without risk,
nothing without waste — spoiling
with jerry-building rash of colliers' houses
an empty landscape.

The same in the Hole —
haste, cobbling, devil-may-care,
charging nature with too much.

One democratic heat for a whole people!
New babbies and sick-unto-death
drawn into the fire-corner.

Our abandoned village underground
one more settlement
for future men to peel away its layers,
understand a buried stratum
of the long struggle.

Chorus

What's he mouthing now?
Is it about the accident?
He's spoken, you know, here in the hospital,
after years of saying nowt . . .

I'm glad you've come,
glad of the comfort,
of the patterns we make,
trailing in and out
to the coffee-machine and the telephone.

I don't want to think on my own
of the broken strands, the raw ends.

Death is not what it was, the one end,
but one more ending
of those that come at break-neck speed.

No-one goes down that pit.
Passages in the rock that he kept
fill up, do they, with unwinding water?
He was glad. He said, 'Good riddance,'
not bothered that it's all to-broken now.

His muckers cast to the four winds —
taken on at Shaw's Carpets,
driving a fork-lift,

coach driver, cab driver, window-cleaner,
double-glazing installer.
Still colliers, and, as they allus were,
high-hand and off-hand with other trades!

Credit where credit's due?
We will not forget?
But who wants the long memories of the Hole?
Toil and dirt, rancour and heat?

Faces lily-white under pit dirt
raced up to this hospital many a time.

Down there a blade sliced off my neighbour's face,
no eyes to see the doctors' make-over.
His wife, sick to the heart,
lived one year after.
He's still alive — for a long time
we knew him by his quiff of black hair.
Now stark white, as he walks out after dark.

It riles me, though, that Eddie missed out,
should have been good words down there
for a quiet mucker, worked his socks off
to keep the Hole near-normal as he could.

Eddie

We tried to keep it normal.
Home from home.
The pump house took out tons
of drowning water
and the fans
batted out foul air.

Most endured. A few felt nervous dread,
born with us, or something on the slate
we couldn't rub clean.

Sorry for the youngsters.
A boy with this fear in's heart and stomach
knows each loose cobble on the route,
each snagging barb in the sharp hedge
where someone's ducked through for a short cut
leaving behind a few shreds of himself.

He'd call on sparrows to hold him back,
his boots in a dead march with other boots.

The ambush waited me ten years.
By my book, it must come.

Chorus

How long was Eddie Safety Officer?
Thirty years? After the accident,
they offered him a surface job. But 'No way!'

Eddie was the last one they got out breathing
and, yes, they'd try him on the safety job.
The last man blotted his copybook, no question!
Our Eddie's books were always straight.
He wrote, you know, a lovely copper-plate.

This week, he's unclammed at last.
As it's been told to me, it's nothing much.

Only that Eddie was trapped alongside
a half Irish boy, very good tempered,

twenty-one just, but Eddie says he had
a family of three little girls already.

The cheerful smashed boy couldn't feel a thing,
chatting on about his dog,
had a soft gift for stories, like turning on a tap.

Eddie, near-death, pelvis broke and both legs —
in pain, he says, worse than bearing a child
(how could he know! but that's his kidding on) —
started cackling at some yarn of Paddy's . . .

And so it caught the rescuers' cocked ear
as an unbearably human sound.
Recalled twice from that part,
where a second fall was overdue,
on tenterhooks, unable to leave,
they gently drew the teeth of those rocks.

This time all got out without more hurt,
except the arc-lights saw Paddy dead,
and in the green light,
Eddie coalblack with their joined blood.

Eddie

Morphine divides me from rottenness,
keeps bodiless hunger fed
with thoughts from the stomach. . .

Dying in due time, at three score and ten.
Hearty old women still stand round,
stood clacking at their gates
when we came home from school.

The same women! The same women, saying
'He dies young!'

How old? Twenty? Twenty-five?
Washed out pinnies bound across
wombs swelled for the third time.
The kicking babby getting ready
to oust the dummied infant from the pram,
to oust the toddler through the garden-gate,
to push us up the hill of school and work. . .

I thought them old —
a day's work in slumped backs, in swollen legs
conducting weariness to the concrete paths.

But now as fresh as daisies, old and young.

Chorus

In at a death, not sure of our job,
we hover near his bed.

We tend dying flowers,
clean out of the locker
dying food.

We think of moving closer,
of holding his hand —
try to remember what was done
in times more regular?

Shall we put to his lips
a tea-spoon of water?
Shall we ask the Sister?

Shall we push forward or hold back?
Push others forward?

His daughter clings to us.

I cling to them.

She knows him least (so she says).

Because I knew him best.

He fixed her plaits,
put Sunday ribbons in her hair.
Today, it's like Mum and Dad dying in one bed.
She's younger today and older.

I'm younger today and older.
It's seeing the two die in one bed,
and of the two he was the tenderer.

Eddie

Women come to a death —
not men if they can help it —
come but keep their distance.

Women, old and young,
with your many uses
and your many usages (though rusty)
use now to ease my passage
with your humming voices,
normally as raucous as rooks.

The last use of long bones is as oars.

The edge holds a rim of gold
that stays for the afternoon shift,
for men to see the light wound up,
and to learn from the hundredth part of it
what temper of day it's been.

While the thick cloth still binds your hand
with my heaped plate steaming in it,
red-hot from the black oven,
I'll tell you what sort of day.

Apart from a few squalls,
it's been a very calm and not too cold,
short winter day.

Chorus

I know he's gone. I go for your hand.
I'm already mangling it!

I can't say what he was.
Better'an me, I know that.
To stand up to him in what he thought right
was to put your hand towards
the white whirr of a fast wheel.

What he held back, I now feel coming,
restless forces outside,
soulless back-and-forth,
hot and cold, angry rushes,
destructive exhaustion.

Thank you for warming my hands
with a carton of coffee.

There go the curtains.
They've started on him.

A few years ago, we laid them out.

I'm trembling with nervous reaction
(that's what they call it), hammered, too,
by lorries bulldozing towards MI,
socking into the roots of this temporary place.

II

CHRISTMAS OUT OF LONDON

23 December

A quarter-inch of frost.
Your reproach keen as frost.
The hill's sun halts half-way.
On the white valley floor,
brakes of dog-rose hooped in
a new thorny durance,
the fat, blood-red rose-hips,
bright gash of Northern skies,
sterile packaged in frost.

24 December

A fierce wren scuffles
in the dark silvered cape
of ivy prising the cliff:
rackets for a living
under a portcullis
of foot-long icicles,
wasting, but resetting
their brittle chimes early,
taut to the wind's finger.

25 December

Rain's white rods prevent feet
across the green threshold.
Green stone-walls, green tree-boles,
tell how much rain washes down
the hill's green boulder:
makes indoor-day a cave
of breath from the oven —
you fussing like a wren,
darting anger about.

BATH CITY SNOW SQUALL

Poetry is a squall of words.
How soon it whitens the track.
Hear from the thrush's stretched throat,
'Alone! Don't look back! Alone!'

How loud the thrush began to shout
by the car-park, 'Don't look back!'
The young tree shaken by its throat,
people stopping and craning back.

What of thrush's wild call in stone town?
Nature strikes back — its blotting squall:
we meet like Yeti in cols of stone,
'Alone! Don't look back! Alone!'

STONE-BREAKING IN FINSBURY

London! London!
I hear your Catechism.
Only one stone way
through London night prism.

Red, orange,
yellow, green,
blue, indigo, violet.

Feet beating stones,
stones beating feet,
slurred down-beat,
light up-beat,
beat it, beat it,
beat it out —
the steel of the shoe-heels,
the sparkles of the feet.

In stone country
we reach water,
splashing to our feet,
waterfalls
of Angel escalators.

Such flow of silver water,
so many paddling,
assuaging dry heat
of the underways,
the glaring passages,
the stone slopes.

Down, down and out,
up, up and out,
into London night,
a causeway for seven colours
of broken Finsbury moon.

Red, orange,
yellow, green,
blue, indigo, violet

dispersing like water
over London stones.

CHOIRMASTER'S REVERIE

In my Choir, a small cat
sitting upright, quite still,
a pointed, insignificant tump
that could be God's thumb,
he wants to show me, thumbs up.

As God walks in the crypt,
his thumb, pushing up,
tells me he's not Up There, but
in the bowels of Christ. 'Old Mole,
can'st work i' the ground so fast?'

The black cat comes in because
it's hot in the Close. The use
of our tiles to cool his rump is one
I would often like to put them to!
Schooling my Choir, I'd like to put
my head to God's cool hand of his floor.

O fellow-creature!

The carver's and the mason's art,
your setting now, is not
more densely thought than your black coat.

But whose thought are you?

On your pelt's glitter
you split light,
toss off rainbows galore!

The bestiary under
the Misericord seats has come to life!

Carolling lover, you came to my Dulwich garden
a few days before we met here.
Why do I trouble?
My Choir could not do your sexy burble
even with your notes in black and white.

Whatever you are, you seem
imperishably so,
supplely now scratching your white belly.

Yours or not, God, he's timeless to me.
See how he scoots, paws skidding!

EARLY SUMMER MORNING IN DULWICH

Two male-mannequin foxes, fluent haunches
draped in apricot designer-fur,
cat-walk the sheds next to The Dog.
I call an animal-lover.
He comes as he is, naked:
'What a glorious colour!'

As sun takes fire again from yesterday's embers,
flash-flames shoot into the air's roseate glow.

Now foxy visitors slope off, now heat gets up,
sweet, nauseous droppings
interfere with garden nosegays.

Next-door's cat, run over, shallowly interred,
dug up and torn in twenty pieces last night.
Lindsay gathers Adonis slowly
in a black bag — curses foxes.

As we search, stupendous stink
marks a new find. Under the hedge,
where she crept from heat, a grey vixen rots.

Lindsay and I, the naked man, now dressed,
feel sorry for the slicked pelt of the corpse,
her long bared teeth.

IF THIS SUMMER LASTS

If this summer lasts
we'll straighten our bones:
sun drying roses,
curing neuroses.

Windows wide at night
let in with warm air
bub, bub, bub, bub, bub,
bubbling from the pub.

Summer's on the boil:
all day in the sun
stretch winter-warped bones,
wake with straightened ones.

We go to bed late,
we get up late-late.
We lift the warm sun
from eyelids at noon.

While this summer lasts,
long sleep, straightened bones:
sun drying roses,
curing neuroses.

ONSET

Summer — in one characteristic burst!
Heat transferred from flesh to flesh,
from lightly-steaming earth
to emblematic breaking bud.

What response can his parents make this year
to the thousand buds on the old-fashioned rose,
each breaking into a striped, scrunched bloom?

Sprung branches are light, dewy obstructions
to the family car manoeuvring out
to start the early hospital run.
They leave a trail of drops across its hard polish.
Each holds a miniature distortion
of womb-like house and garden,
then burns off.

Jonathon's eyes, dryly fixed on the ward's walls,
won't come to terms with present, future or past.

He cold-shoulders them, won't walk
in the old Asylum grounds
where modern plantings sizzle.

Distractedly, they think of normal heat-waves —
of hay-feverish mown lawns,
after-supper walking the dog,
the heat still in the collie's coat.

Will normality come?
It could be a year round
before he forgets the garden chairs,

cushions soaked in a snap storm,
before the disturbed hornet,
missionary from its eaves nest,
leaves its innocent hard sting
in her shoulder's sunburned tissue.

What sudden onset this year, this summer?
A grown-boy's high screams.

Hearts like a summer ice-house.

In this heat, cold, clasped hands.

SERIOUS BREAKDOWN
OF A NINETEEN YEAR OLD

'To Rosalind and John a son',
but much later a miscarriage of Jonathon,
who wants to give up his nineteen years.

To these parents this,
to this boy this,
to these parents,
to this boy,
to these,
to this,
to —

It has come to no words —
not nineteen, not one.
John and Rosalind nod to the hard slap
of midwifery, of electricity.
Jonathon must be re-born.

He has been screaming. He refused a sup of water
for forty-eight hours. He drinks.

Later, they take him home, starting again
as if Jonathon was their first born.

They must not swaddle the adult — must not
go up the stairs too often (the old stairs).

They wait downstairs for screams, for too quiet —
must not go up to see for a cot-death.

They plan to bring him back, to birth-place,
to birth people, to his nineteen years —

to,
to this,
to these,
to this boy,
to these parents
to this boy this
to these parents this

to Jonathon, a birth.

PLAIN SPEAKER

Your cruelty's a vein in marble,
would not be yourself without that dark flaw.
Do you know it? Do you know why?
You ask, 'What's that fool weeping for?'

Rough tongue scrapes off tawdry gilding,
rasps down to each life's naked grain.
No man? No child? What else is missing?
Such stimulation of numbed pain!

You speak out like a tranced Sibyl.
Narcotist! You once meant our good.
Sister to the Mother at Delphi:
let dooms be known, if not understood!

How often have we been like this?
Mother and daughter. Pity-proof.
Shown steel between us in a closed room,
held less close to the throat, plain truth?

SEPTEMBER

A big, soft wind,
blunt but heavy,
weighs down the trees' branches,
recalls sea-waves loosening land.

Wind, like a ton of water,
slowly, from shelf to shelf,
weighs down the trees' branches.

The slow uprising draught
unsettles a sea of leaves.
Sequential waves of leaves wash here,
wash up in darkness here.

Her life, loosened, falling,
like a leaf's wambling fall:
I listen for her sleep and hear shore sounds;
the wind, like water, combs all it finds.

Her thin mewl, then, like a grated keel,
a gull's mew in the night:
a wild, difficult sound.

Not compliance, not protest —
for death, against death —
a human, wilderness sound.

An exact sound pierces the vague mass
of soft wind, that irresistibly, like water,
fills up the night's globe.

I'D BUILD A WILLOW CABIN AT YOUR GATE

Of course, there is a difference this year —
Autumn conspiracy for staying on.
Tourists sit it out in London pavement cafes.
Londoners too relax in the open air.

Of course, it's a mistake, lacuna, Indian Summer.
It can't last.
The North (where you come from)
is betrayed in its green coat
by sudden drives of snow,
surprising at first,
but as the blizzard grows monstrous,
crams all parts and blots them out,
chilled hearts in the North
grow inured to the long cold.

By contrast, London's calm, generous
(today, hotter than Madrid)
and here we are:
the forecast for your life,
'Only a few weeks more,'
embowered in this freak of mellow weather.

The daily sun is hot by ten o'clock.
The fragile living holds and holds,
as if, where Death knows he has us,
we set our caps and woo like captive doves.

'I'd build a willow cabin at your gate.'
All day we sit it out, and how kindly
the wattled walls, that suit love at its end
allow the passage of the last warm sun.

The cabin is crowded by two women,
one in her nightie, one in summer clothes.

A perilous squat we hold on his fenced land.
But neither death nor frost
are eager in nineteen-ninety-six.

In a clement pastoral of all-day sun,
we chat and wait for pressure to fall.

The air will cool and bite in with the darkness
to this hovel as leaky as a sieve.
Our garden-house is simply a petition:
'To our Master, open before the winter
your house stronger than bricks and mortar.'

TWO WOMEN

Our manfriend, Death, in earnest joins us now,
makes a tight circle, edging by turns to both.
Good conversation? Yes.
But, like all visitors to the dying,
interpolates his own concerns and needs,
not hearing centred meanings, retrospects.
He loves his own voice, intolls male boom
into significant talk, hogging it.

A tactile male,
he lays a long thigh to each of us.
Its melting wax threatens a seal.

When he touches your hand or arm,
I don't like it.
A chatty, insinuating, controlling man,
who thinks he's God's gift to two women.

I look at the clock and say,
'I'll get lunch now,
then she'll have her rest.'
His hot, eager body's in a bustle at once,
'I'll help you,' he says.

MOTHER AT THE LAST

Mother, at the last
mewling for life-past,
for present sick pain,
life-last stares aghast
at life-lost, no gain,
denies life hand-fast,
body's and soul's joint state,
life-whole, sound past,
life you would not abate.

Last hours
mewl for past hours.
Pain for gain of good years
sources these tears.
Failed steps refer
to steps that unerr.
Hands shake with sick will,
recall speed, skill.
Attrition is defined
by fed body, mind.

All of life-past
line up at life-last,
life lived, life given
in youth,
minute by minute, built
and, water and wind-proof,
lived in, in truth.

Deny that you roofed over time,
and lived sound in the shelter of hours?
You who lived merry,

sound in the shelter of hours,
die sorry.

Aghast at life-last,
you loved life-lost, life-past.

Pain counts life-long a gain.

INCIDENT ON THE THIRD STOREY

On the one hand, this is the world we know:
the slightly unpredictable seasons,
the slow, insidious, slant fall of snow
like torn tissues fluttered past glazed prisons.
On the other hand, the confidence we show
in clock-face time, wired for vision and sound,
is now a sham: all neat divisions go,
passed down to those below stamping the white ground.
Fathers calling to sons skidding in snow,
that floats down its expected change early
but not too early, live in a world they know,
or think they know, that here stops finally.
So not too soon the blanketing of snow,
like, when you die, switching off your radio.

LIFE

You watch your mother changing towards death.
Then mother and death are the same dun shade.

It finishes with confluence, for how can we
express him except in her surprised rictus?

Death is so — as she is now — recognised stranger.

But dying is the river as we go along, living;
soon becoming the familiar medium.
We go along with it,
we go along with the doctors' forecasts,
we adapt, we camouflage
(living properties and naturally
concerned with survival).

We live through dying, adjust continually,
not to be caught by pity or by death.

Death is also a chameleon,
picked out from distracting surroundings
by foreknowledge and concentration.

By his property of change and ours also,
we know his power and his authority.

His strangeness continues to be ourselves
before and when we assume our latest change.

When we were young,
was death a distant obelisk,
monumental as the yew among trees?

We soon learn that changeful weeks of intimate dying
are not the stones we put up after.

New confluences between 'living' and 'dead' —
a new chain of mathematics,
climbing all the way, or golden cascade from the centre,
showering relationship on us.
We must revise ideas of 'living matter'.

But still the layman knew when you were dead:
cheeks wash-leather, no bubble of yeasty blood.

During your slow, foreseen dying, you found new life,
showed that dying is living, having its own excitement,
arrogance, power to draw an audience . . .

Flushed up, oratorical, experimental with ideas and people:
it seemed the energy-burst would go on
until the last Bunsen cooled, until the lab.
was shut up with its fumose atmosphere.

OVER THE EDGE

I should have bathed your face more. Each time I did it
the luke-warm animal sponge flattered your flesh a little,
freshened it and disencrusted it of the dry traces
of medicine around your mouth, or muzzle as it seemed.

It was not the flesh responding, but your heart,
rising to the rhythm of closeness, of involvement,
briefly distancing the truth (which made you furious
and made you disdainfully withdraw into yourself)
that, from daughter to mother, on what should be a fizzing
electric arc, no love, just anxious concern, was passed.

How I hurried you to your death, dragged you to its gulf,
knew at every point that, if I loved, I could not bear this,
felt relief when the cleft stick of your illness lost its grip
on me, pinned you down to not a single painless moment.

Then, when I had to dispose your bruised limbs,
already melting into the last form of flesh
(the bed already sodden, the last animal hole),
you said, despairingly, 'More gentle'.
In your agony, 'You are a murderess,' you said –
that was on Christmas Day – and told me,
'Don't call me Mother.'
The less accusing words arrested me ('more gentle').

On the one hand, you asked the wholly impracticable,
because I could not move you without great pain
for you and despair for me, or without fear of cracking
a limb, the pelvis, or the spine, so thin to breaking
you seemed; but, on the other hand, you wanted my heart
to be more gentle, more reluctant to let you go,

you knew that, even wincing at your pain,
flinching from more damage to your flesh,
which tore like tissue paper,
the urgency in my hands pushed you over the edge.

GRIEF

For weeks and months, I think that you have gone.
Nothing that reminds me of you hurts me,
not caught out by your voice,
not spooked, at first, by the contraptions in the hallway,
medicines, too, lined up for disposal, melancholy
owl-pellets under the bed, where odd pills, hair-grips
have become coated in fluff.

At first, I don't see what grips me,
but then I do see it: the air between objects
in these top-storey rooms where you died from day to day
is thickly enamelled with overlapping pictures
of what was done; what you did for and to yourself;
what we did for you and to you; little, bright images
of patience and agony, like the lives of the saints;
an overlap of paillettes; exactly the same, as when,
with eyes open in waking dream, I've often hundreds
of V-incised serpents, intertwined and slowly shifting,
filling what should be the dull space between things.

You have gone, consuming yourself completely. It took
all your remaining kindness towards life, and rationality.
When those thinned and cracked, it didn't matter.
You had finished.

But when will these images be worn out, or suspended:
the grimace on a tall skeleton, as the black nurse hugged
you out of the bath; you slowly cleansing your anus
with single tissues; you hefting to your lips dull porridge
of liquidised lentils, spuds and carrots; you calling
for sick-bowls, for towels and tissues, succeeding

in never sullying with your leaky body
linen that must be washed;
you scowling at the mirror we must pass;
you tearing half the skin off your neck in a fall
against the metal-armed commode,
showing that your defence against bruising and flaying
the whole surface was no more than tissue-paper?

It should be no surprise that objects
linked with your death, which apologetic people
hauled away so quickly (your slight corpse, too,
'Close the door, so you don't need to see it pass')
seemed harmless, and, for weeks and months,
it seemed you had gone with them, cleared the decks.

But mind, haunting you with entrapment nightmares,
with the fear of fire and live-burial,
waking you, then, to another
experiment of understanding,
is our best and worst companion,
to live with while we live.

IV

CHANGE

Not much to look at, the mining village
swops sun-flash with MI speedway —
just now, it lost its reason for being,
its long tap-root, but goes on, jumbled hopes
not simmered down, not ready to revert
to the simpler statement — Empty Country,
a short car-drive away, each little hill
cobbed with a stone barn.

In the bleak pub, try Alf's tetchy recall
of when the Pit, brand-new, 'fully mechanised',
first began its steady flexing of muscle,
its heart-of-the-earth compulsive rhythm
forcing a black lava-stream up and out,
smoking wagons clanking, then, through farmland,
a slow, dusty, tarry, spreading change,
that women said, 'got into ev'rything',
but slowly, so that, when Alf went down, aged
fourteen, the margins of the pit in May
were oak-woods with mirage of bluebells,
new shale paths were strewn with bunches babies
let fall from high, creaking prams of that time,
larks were drilling above the pit-head track,
rookeries flapping in lazy alarm
at thumps from the new township underground.
Alf can't say why the oak-woods rotted,
rookeries degenerated,
and soon the Hole's raw practice became to him
as immemorial as farming ways.

But now Alf's recall of young days has sunk
to a deep sediment. An old man's self-

soothing story, with plot (and words, too)
as old as the Bible — heroes and bastards,
Good Samaritans, wise and unwise virgins,
his own part as King Solomon, wise steward,
or, further back, the young David against
bone-headed Goliaths of management —
starts to stutter in angry denial:
'Continual upset', 'Interference';
a shaming confusion churns and blacks out
memories he wants to order. He gags on
Maggie and Arthur in one asthmatic whoop.

The end sticks in Alf's craw like the death
of a free-fisted Dad (like Alf's Dad's death).
A bugger in all ways — hot, filthy work,
fair skin scored, welted, bruised all colours
by the tussle, all-in wrestling with angry rock,
pent up two thousand feet under, listening,
not knowing what it might do next, the Hole
was a second Dad to Alf. That sums it up.
In the front room, Alf's tears sizzled on Dad's hands
laid out on his black chest by the Co-op.
Alf's Dad was a productive force. Alf
owed it all to Dad — sperm, grub, pence, fear.
The Hole was such another patriarch.

Alf sucks his ventilator and rallies.
At the end, change came faster, distracted
attention from closure, 'as was meant, tha' knows.'

The pit stopped work, became a sulking sump,
will pucker a house-plot or piece of road
towards its dark, sweaty emptiness –
but not often, and mainly forgotten.

So is that all? As nomad children, we knew
of moorland shafts left over from old times.
And that was 'a'right': the curve of change
roughly matched the shape of lives –
or, between fractures, a long respite –
Grandad's skills were redundant, not Grandson's.

Now lads, who worked just long enough to strut
like colliers, come out at twenty.
The site is levelled, the village
is rid of the black Demon in its heart:
the quaking earth, the grinding HGVs,
doors shuttering as shifts come off and on,
the loud street greetings and street wrangles.
The village is leached, pale and subdued.
People watch indifferently
as gaps are blocked with pre-fab hangers –
for warehouses, for factories? Rumours
hang on the dark source of this supply.

Men and women cross a barrier, talk.
There's new concern about 'the pitch we've reached'.
How to recover our own slow rhythms
is a heavy question the speeded up fever
of heart's desires can't answer.

Spare afternoons, villagers in new cars
bought with Redundancy, cruise Empty Country.

RESOLUTIONS

North Yorkshire Moors, April 1997

To follow the sky's one cloud —
a long-necked goose —
and not to sleep in one bed twice.

To set my face from your shrivelled ghost, Autumn,
and from yours, Winter of Death.

To serve no-one — freed Ariel —
to knuckle down to no Monopolist.

To take a bed and breakfast pilgrimage:
to know, April, your 'shoures soote', or, better still,
day-long sunshine, lark's high drill,
yellow-hammer's gold-streaked hedge-hop.

To make the frayed coast, and to resist
the sea's long pull at toothsome rock.

To take a look, but turn my back on moors,
where ashes of heather smoulder.

To find a roof in pasture valleys
where in steep fields gorse-bushes
are rocks on fire, Easter lilies
crowd the field-margins and copses.

To move on, but to ignore all signs and distances,
all failures to arrive or leave on time.

To give all walkers, 'Good morning',
'Good afternoon', 'Goodnight':
to halve nothing but miles to my new bed.